SABOTAGED & DEFEATED

A Final Glimpse

Part One: Bath - Evercreech

FURTHER PRE & POST CLOSURE VIEWS ON THE SOMERSET & DORSET

Jeffery Grayer

NOODLE N.B. BOOKS

ISBN 978-1-906419-90-5

Printed in England by The Information Press.

First published in 2012 by Kevin Robertson under the **NOODLE BOOKS** imprint
PO Box 279
Corhampton
SOUTHAMPTON
SO32 3ZX

www.noodlebooks.co.uk

Above - *A sepia tinted view taken from the parkland of Midford Castle with the sunshine breaking through the fog to illuminate the passage of the Somerset & Dorset railway through this particularly attractive stretch of the line. (BIT)*

Frontispiece *- From the top of the Long Arch bridge at Midford the line heads away towards Bath under stormy skies in this March 1966 view. (BIT)*

CONTENTS

Front Cover Top *- 34057 "Biggin Hill" makes its way tender first light engine to Evercreech Junction to take over, in tandem with classmate 34006 "Bude", the LCGB special of March 5th 1966. It is seen here passing a lineside workman just to the south of Radstock, the dirt batch of Clandown Colliery being visible in the background. (JG)*

Front Cover Lower *- A mournful sight as a coffin bedecked with a cross of yellow flowers and bearing the legend "S&D Died Today" is loaded on board the last up service train at Evercreech Junction on 5th March 1966. In the absence of a brass band a loudspeaker played "John Brown's Body" as the Stationmaster Alexander Stowe and three of his staff, all sporting purple mourning ribbons in their buttonholes, gently lowered the coffin into the Guards Van. It travelled to the next stop at Evercreech New where it was offloaded and ceremonially placed into a waiting hearse. (BIT)*

Top - *A Hymek runs up the line past a brake van parked underneath the loading gauge on a siding to the south of Binegar station to collect its train before returning to Radstock in the spring of 1968. Notice a sack of coal and associated coal stack in the yard which was still used by the local coal merchant at this time. (JL)*

INTRODUCTION

TRAIN SERVICE

A third volume of "**Sabotaged & Defeated**" – surely not!

Little did I think that when, after a long struggle to get the first volume published in 2006, involving rejections from some dozen publishers, that the title would run to a second let alone a third outing. Prompted by the success of the second volume "**Sabotaged & Defeated – Revisited**" I determined that such was the interest for all things "S&D" that a third volume might meet with similar approval. Mindful of "killing the goose that lays the golden egg" this will be my final look at the subject. Again, some hitherto unseen photographic gems have been uncovered from a variety of sources to complement coverage of the line displayed in the first two books.

I would like to thank particularly Derek Fear, whose photographic collection I have again plundered and without whose foresight many of these views would have remained unphotographed in colour. I would also like to thank Dan Brown of "**Bath in Time**" whose website of the same name I can thoroughly commend to all those seeking historic images of the Bath area. Geoff Plumb, John Lakey and Peter Russell have again also allowed me to dip into their collections, their

Top - *A green enamel sign formerly located above the timetable poster board at Bailey Gate station. (JG)*
Bottom - *Railwaymen pose in front of 80043 forming the 16:25 departure from Bath on the last day of normal service trains, Saturday 5th March 1966. The well filled carriages were packed with enthusiasts taking a final ride on the line. The headboard on the front of the locomotive reads "Farewell S&D". (BIT)*

pictures being supplemented by the few remaining images that I personally took of the line in post-closure days. I would also like to thank Ian Trotter, whose shots of the Somervale Coaches vehicles both before and after termination of their contract to run the rail replacement bus service have been included. Thanks also go to Mark Shore and Martin Sinfield who walked the line in 1972 and recorded their walk on film. Finally many thanks go to various contributors to the excellent "S&D Telegraph", the journal of the Somerset & Dorset Railway Heritage Trust based at Midsomer Norton station, who have permitted me access to their unique shots.

I have consciously tried to illustrate the railway in its landscape setting in this volume, where possible, as the contrasting scenery and topography of the route was an important element in its enduring attraction. This is particularly true of the countryside around Midford which receives considerable coverage here. The layout of Part 1 is geographically based journeying in traditional fashion from north to south from Bath to Evercreech. Part 2 covers the Highbridge branch and the route from Evercreech Junction to Bournemouth. A few minor diversions from the S&D are included in Volume 1 to cover the nearby Frome-Radstock branch - so vital to ensuring the continued exit for Radstock coal once the North Somerset line had closed, together with the associated Kilmersdon colliery, one of the final trio of pits operating in the North Somerset coalfield. The Midland exit from Bath also receives further coverage. The juxtaposition of views of the line in operation with those taken after closure and during the demolition process brings home in a dramatic pictorial fashion the waste of resources and destruction of infrastructure which occurs when a railway route is closed.

Photographic acknowledgements – Derek Fear (DF), John Lakey (JL), Peter Russell (PR), Mark Shore (MSH), Martin Sinfield (MSI), Bath in Time (BIT), Simon Castens (SC), Geoff Plumb (GP), John Chalcraft (RP), Somerset & Dorset Railway Heritage Trust (SDRHT), Graeme Bickerdyke (GB), Nick McCameley (NMcC), Chris Newman (CN), George Woods (GW), Chris Chandler (CC), Colin Brack (CB), Mike Couchman (MC), Martin Body (MB), Tim Chapman (TC).

A 1960's view of the exterior of the impressive façade of Green Park station enhanced by a variety of cars of the period parked on the forecourt. (JG)

Jeffery Grayer
Somerset 2012

BATH GREEN PARK

Top - *An interior shot of the Booking Hall taken in 1964 displaying the Arrival/Departure indicator board on the right. The chalk board positioned in front of the indicator carries the message "......Train service alterations..." dealing with changes to the timings of a Templecombe service. (BIT)*

Bottom - *A 1964 view from the buffer stops looking out over a seemingly deserted Green Park station. The station often exhibited an almost sabbatarian calm with considerable lulls in traffic between departing and arriving services. (BIT)*

Next page - *A 1964 view of a gas lamp standard and nameboard at Green Park. The presence of gas lighting added a nocturnal glow to an already atmospheric location at night. (BIT)*

BATH
BATH
GREEN PARK

The magnificent train shed, opened in 1870, is well displayed in this 1964 view. Just four passengers are in evidence. (BIT)

Top - *The rundown of the S&D started at the end of the 1962 Summer timetable. A welcoming crowd turned out to witness "Evening Star" arriving at Green Park station with the last "Pines Express" on 8th September - there were to be no more "Pines" or holiday trains on the S&D thereafter. Ironically the 9F was to be transferred back to the S&D in the summer of 1963, together with 92224, even though there were only 3 and 4 coach local trains for them to haul. As they were too long to be turned on the turntable at Evercreech Junction this effectively precluded their use on freight duties. (JL)*

Bottom - *Two days later "Evening Star" is seen on shed at Green Park. It had been specially transferred to the S&D in lieu of 92210 in August so it could work both the final up and down "Pines Express". (RP)*

Opposite - *Synonymous with the S&D were the Fowler 7F 2-8-0s constructed especially for the line in two batches. 53806, one of the second batch, is seen here at Green Park in September 1963. This locomotive was withdrawn in January 1964. (RP)*

53806
82F

Left - *80138 rolls into Green Park with a service from Templecombe on 25th May 1965. A waiting Royal Mail Morris Minor van stands ready underneath the large Bonded Stores notice to receive the incoming mails, a scene now gone from the railways of this country. (RP).*

Above - *On the 7th December 1965 75072 had brought in the 11:46 service from Bournemouth and D121 coupled up to the rear of the train to take it on to Bristol, its final destination. Seven minutes were allowed in the timetable on Mondays – Fridays between arrival and departure from Bath. (DF)*

Opposite bottom - *Filthy BR Standard 5MT 4-6-0 No. 73001 has the road and is ready to go as it waits the "rightaway" from Bath Green Park station with the 09:53 to Bournemouth West. With just under four months until closure, things are looking pretty run down on a wet and miserable Thursday 23rd December 1965. (GP)*

Top - *82004 sets out with the virtually empty one coach 18:05 Binegar local service on 31st August 1965. (DF)*

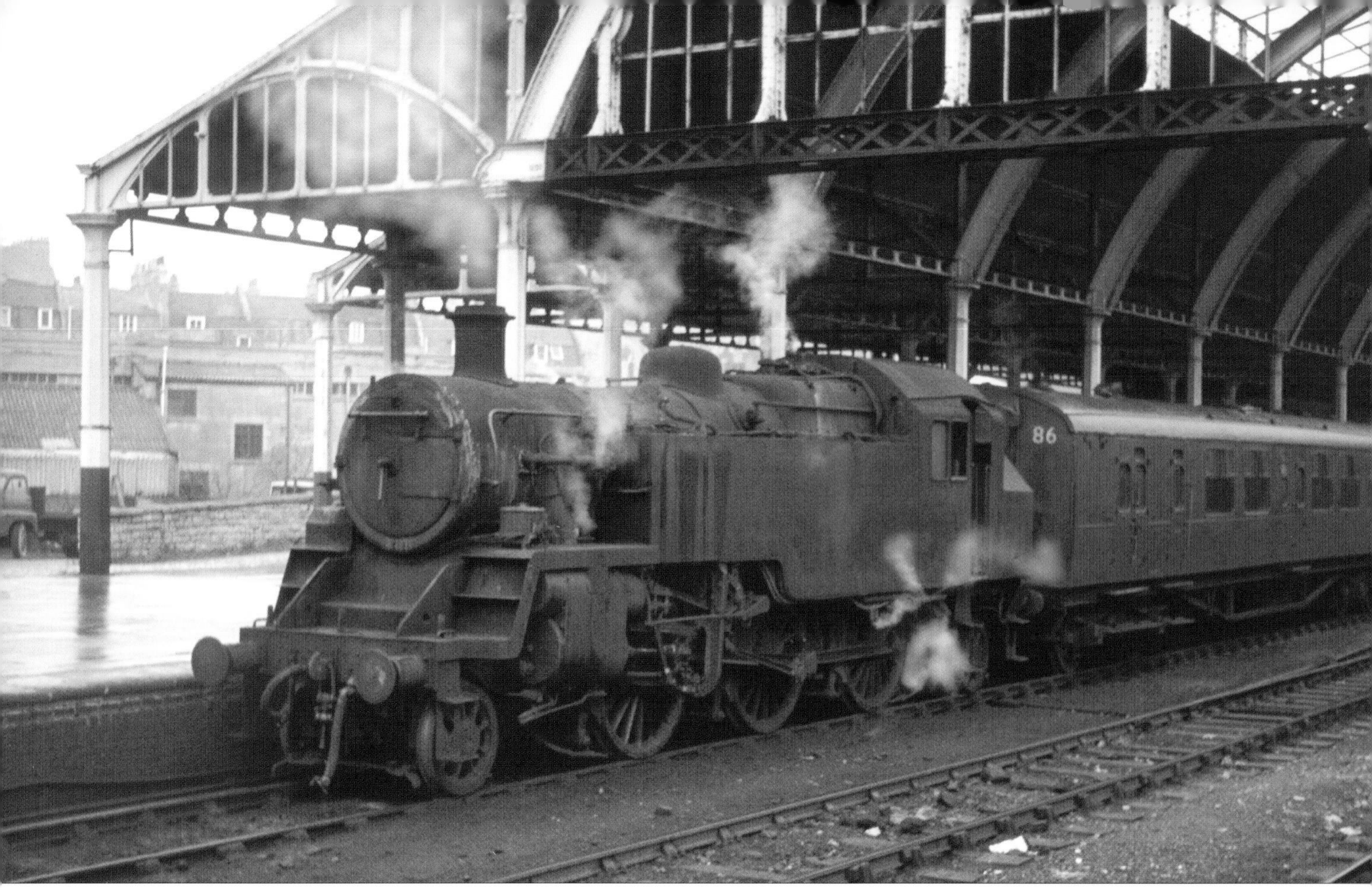

Top - *Filthy dirty and almost unidentifiable BR Standard 3MT 2-6-2T No. 82001 stands in the platform at Bath Green Park station with a rake of empty SR coaches which it is about to take out to the sidings, on a miserable Thursday 23rd December 1965. (GP)*

This page, bottom - *D17 takes up the coaching stock from one of the middle roads which will form a service to Bristol via Mangotsfield on Friday 3rd December 1965. At this time there were just seven daily departures on Mondays – Fridays from Bath on this route. (DF)*

Top - *Simmering under Green Park's impressive overall roof is a very woebegone 76026 having just arrived with the 16:18 service from Templecombe on 4th March 1966 during the currency of the "Emergency Timetable." (DF)*

Bottom - *A specially "bulled up" 8F 48706 at the head of the returning Great Western Society special enters Green Park station on March 5th 1966. (DF)*

Top - *One track has already been removed in this 1966 view of the approach to Green Park station, the remaining tracks in the station area and locomotive depot being lifted in January 1967. (SDRHT)*

Bottom - *With all tracks removed the station awaits its new role as car parking, temporary fencing having been erected on the far platform.*

Top - *A general view of the exit road from Bath Green Park shed, taken on 31st March 1966, less than a month after closure of the line, looking towards Bath Junction. The shed area has been cleared of dumped engines leaving just an old sludge tender and some mineral wagons and* ***(bottom)*** *a few ex-GWR 'Toad' brakevans appear on the right as we look back towards the station and the deserted Midland shed. In the two weeks following closure locomotives were towed away from Green Park by a variety of diesel locomotives including Peak D15 and Hymek D7043 but Ivatt tank 41283 is known to have been steamed for shunting stock up to 17th March probably making it the last steam locomotive to have worked on the Western Region. (Both: GP)*

Top - *80059 parked on the withdrawn siding outside the Midland shed at Green Park on 2nd January 1966, This Standard tank had been taken out of service the previous month. (DF)*

Bottom - *82004 comes off shed on 1st September 1965. Based at Bath since October 1959 this Standard Class 3 was to be withdrawn the month after this view was taken. (DF)*

***Top** - Having backed out of the platform, by means of the central run round road, 75072 waits to enter the shed on 9th October 1965 after having brought in the 11:46 service from Bournemouth. (DF)*

***Bottom** - 8F 48706 is seen against the backdrop of the water softening tower at Bath on 23rd September 1965. This 8F was to last in service until closure of the S&D a few months later. (DF)*

LCGB
35028
LCGB THE SOMERSET & DORSET RAIL TOUR
2nd - SPECIAL EXCURSION
The Locomotive Club of Great Britain
SOMERSET & DORSET RAIL TOUR
(C.M.1883) Sat. 5th., March 1966
WATERLOO-SALISBURY-TEMPLECOMBE
EVERCREECH JCT.-HIGHBRIDGE-
EVERCREECH JCT.BATH GREEN PARK
BLANDFORD FORUM-BOURNEMOUTH C.
BASINGSTOKE- WATERLOO.
(S) For conditions see over
0044
0044

Opposite top - *The shunter with his pole hitches a ride on an extremely unkempt Pannier tank. The other WR influence seen in the background, a maroon liveried 'Western' hydraulic in the form of D1031 ' Western Marksman', is decidedly cleaner.*

Opposite bottom - *Merchant Navy pacific 35028 "Clan Line" is seen at the head of the RCTS "Somerset & Dorset Farewell" railtour on 6th March 1966 before departure from London Waterloo. The Bulleid headed the train to Broadstone and up the S&D to Templecombe No.2 Junction whence the train was taken over by a brace of Ivatt tanks for the journey to Highbridge. 35028 returned the train from Templecombe to Waterloo via the LSWR mainline. (GW)*

This page - *A magnificent sight on Green Park shed on March 5th 1966 as a pair of unrebuilt Bulleid Pacifics wait to resume haulage of the LCGB "Somerset & Dorset Rail Tour". They had earlier brought in the special from Evercreech Junction and after approximately an hour at Bath would take out the special leaving at 16:07 to Bournemouth Central whence 35028 would take over for the journey to London arriving some 90 minutes late due to signal checks experienced on the mainline and additional photographic stops having been made on the S&D. (GW)*

53801
53801

48444

Opposite top - *This rather sad view shows a withdrawn 53801 awaiting the end on the scrapline at Crewe in September 1961. The first of the eleven strong class had been withdrawn back in May 1959 but the final member survived until September 1964, 53801 being withdrawn in June 1961. Fortunately two examples have been preserved. Curiously, it is accompanied by one of the WD 2-8-0s, two examples of which were tried on the S&D by the Western Region as a possible replacement for the 7Fs in 1958/59. They failed abysmally in this task, and the 7Fs carried on until the WR had virtually eradicated freight on the line. (JG)*

Opposite bottom - *48444 waits on shed in its capacity as "spare" to cover any locomotive failures on 2nd January 1966. This locomotive was withdrawn the following month and was subsequently scrapped at Cashmore's of Newport. The 8Fs had been drafted onto the S&D from 1961 to replace the 7Fs which began to be withdrawn from 1959 onwards, and became the final heavy goods locomotives on the line. The Western Region had failed to find a suitable replacement from its own resources, as described above. (DF)*

Right - *In the gloom of the wooden S&D shed at Bath 75076 is glimpsed on 2nd January 1966. 48760 with headlamp still lit can be seen on the adjacent road. (DF)*

Bottom - *Within the stone built Midland shed on 1st January 1966 Jinty 47544 stands condemned beneath a smoke hood keeping company with pannier tank 3681 and fellow Jinty 47506 which would both somehow soldier on until the end in March. (DF)*

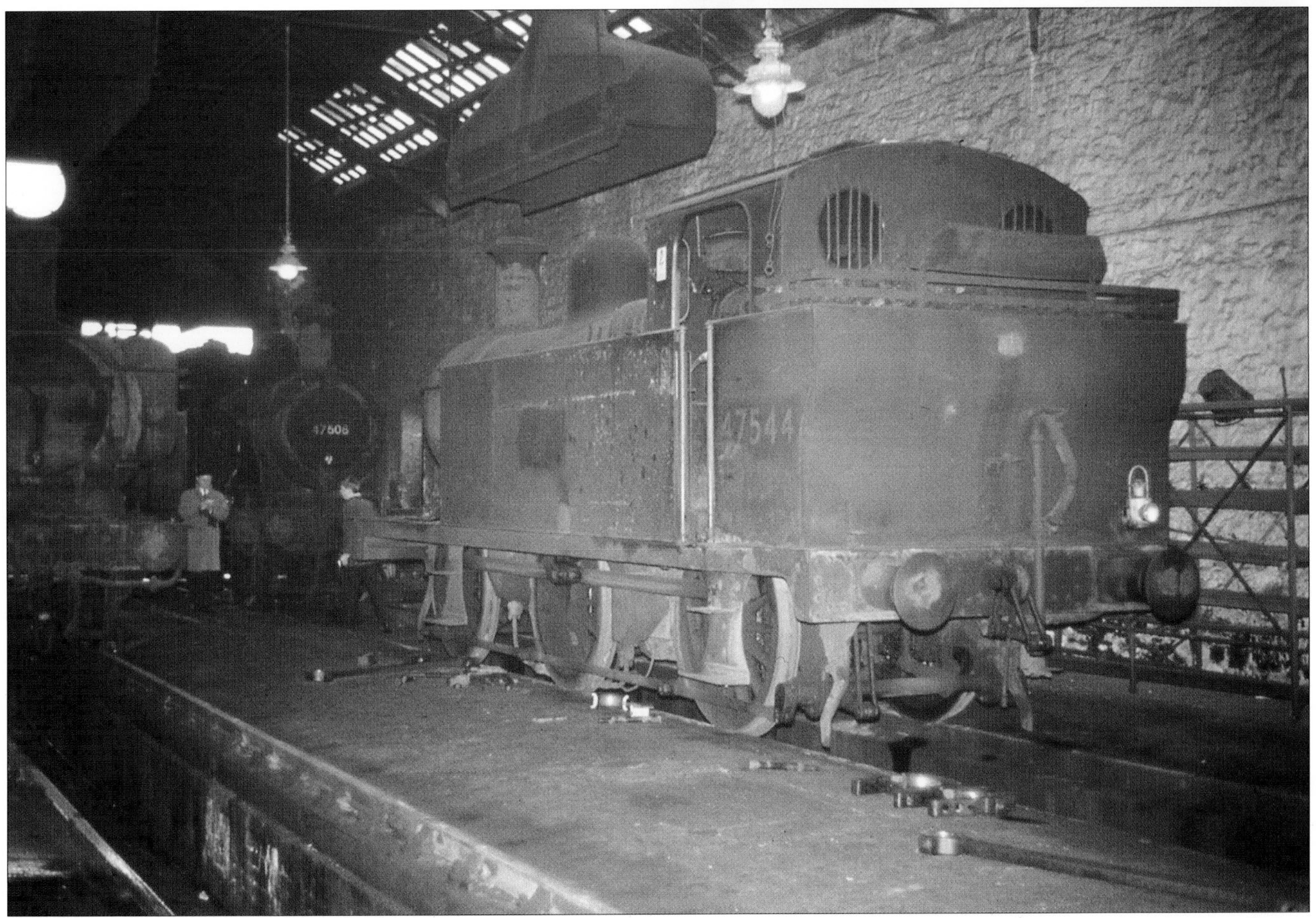

80134

Previous page - *Still plenty of steam activity on shed in this view taken on 23rd September 1965. In evidence are Stanier 8F 48706 together with Standard tanks 80059 and 80134. (DF)*

This page, top - *A scene of utter devastation showing the remains of Green Park shed, the demolition of which was completed in May 1967. A line of trucks can be seen on the former mainline to the right whilst a solitary siding leads diagonally across the site. The circular base seen to the right marks the position of one of the water softening plant towers. (JG)*

BATH JUNCTION

Left - *This view of the former Bath Junction dates from 17th August 1972 and reveals that the trackwork here has been reduced to just a single line which had provided access for the remaining regular freight service to Bath Midland Bridge Road goods yard and Bath gasworks until May the previous year. Occasional freight was still dealt with until closure of the whole route from Mangotsfield to Bath on 20th April 1972, track lifting beginning the following month. (MSH)*

***Top -** Three contractors hold up the former box plate during the demolition of Bath Junction signalbox in 1967. (Roy Brown courtesy SDRHT)*

***Bottom -** About to pass over the level crossing to the west of the closed Weston station in the suburbs of Bath, 82001, running bunker first, brings in a service from Bristol on 2nd December 1965. (DF)*

WESTON

WARMLEY

Opposite top - *Judging by the indentations in the ballast, track and sleepers have only recently been removed in this view of Warmley station looking south. Tracklifting on the Mangotsfield to Bath section began in May 1972 following closure of the line to freight the previous month. (JG)*

Opposite bottom - *Although the crossing gates seen above have gone the signalbox at Warmley looks smart today in a fresh coat of paint. The platforms here are busy again with walkers and cyclists stopping for refreshment. (JG)*

Right - *View looking towards Staple Hill tunnel with the platforms of the former station still in evidence in the deep cutting. (JG)*

Bottom - *A derelict looking Fishponds seen after cessation of freight services to Bath as witnessed by the rusting track. Stopping Passenger services through here finished in 1966 although the route continued to be used by trains from Bristol to the Midlands and North until 3rd January 1970. (JG)*

STAPLE HILL

FISHPONDS

EXIT FROM BATH

Bridge No.1 which took the S&D across the main A4 road from Bath to Bristol (also known as the Red House Bridge) is seen during the course of demolition on May 4th 1969. A road crane, on hire from the local firm of Sparrows, was used together with a flat bed lorry to remove the cast iron spans. The gasholders of the former Bath Gaslight & Coke Co. are prominent on the left of the main picture. (CC)

No10
e to give
CAUTION
DEMOLITION

In winter sunshine 8F 48706 heads the Great Western Society special of 5th March 1966 up the bank from Bath Junction towards the overbridge that crosses the GW mainline. A lone cameraman stands on Bellott's Road bridge which conveniently parallels the rail bridge at this point. (JG)

The special seen above climbs the 1 in 50 grade towards Devonshire Tunnel with its train of well filled maroon coaching stock. No doubt the householders whose washing is seen hanging out to dry in the gardens on the left of the picture will welcome the imminent demise of the line and an end to smuts disfiguring their pristine sheets ! (JG)

82030

Previous page top - *Having just departed from Bath at 09:53, 73001 has passed Bath Junction and crossed over the Great Western main line and has now opened up for the 1 in 50 climb to Devonshire and Combe Down tunnels as it makes its way towards Bournemouth on Thursday 23rd December 1965. (GP)*

Previous page bottom - *82030 attacks the grade from Bath Junction on the 17th November 1965 with the 13:10 service to Templecombe. (DF)*

This page - *Seldom photographed is the line in the context of its urban setting and this view of the bridge spanning Monksdale Road is unusual. Taken in the last month of the line's life it is an interesting record particularly as the bridge was demolished in 1973. Today the balance is being redressed by the provision of a new road crossing for the cycle and footpath which will link Bath via the Two Tunnels project to Midford and beyond utilizing the old trackbed. Note the old road sign on the left warning of a low bridge and narrow road surmounted by a red warning triangle. (JG)*

DEVONSHIRE TUNNEL

Top - *A low sun combined with steep cutting sides always made this a difficult location to film on the descent from Devonshire tunnel into Bath. A Standard tank has charge of the 12:05 service from Templecombe on 26th October 1965. (DF)*

Bottom - *A 1967 view of the track becoming increasingly weed infested following a year of disuse. The track removal gangs would reach this spot at the south end of Devonshire tunnel in the spring of 1968. (JG)*

Next page - *The delightful Lyncombe Vale with a lone Ivatt tank making its steady way along the single line section from Bath Junction to Midford in early 1966. Note the smoke haze drifting up from the mouth of Devonshire Tunnel on the left. (JG)*

COMBE DOWN TUNNEL

Previous page top - *Bridge No.13, otherwise known as Moger's Bridge, at 1 mile 73.5 chains from Bath Junction on the curving approach to the northern portal of Combe Down tunnel is seen in 1967. This masonry arch lined with blue brick carried an occupation road and footpath over the line. (JG)*

Previous page bottom - *In its attractive sylvan setting this view of the northern portal of Combe Down tunnel taken in the 1970s will be transformed with the completion of the Two Tunnels Greenway project designed to provide a foot and cyclepath from Bath through the tunnel to connect with that already in service at Midford. (JG)*

Above - *The northern portal of the tunnel and immaculate permanent way seen on the last afternoon of service trains, March 5th 1966, betrays no suggestion of the line's imminent demise. (JG)*

Next three pages - *Three stunning images of the interior of the mile long Combe Down tunnel showing that the very low roof was composed mainly of natural rock with brick arch supports provided in places. (All: GB)*

Opposite top - *Near the northern end an abrupt change in section sees the roof rise by several feet.*

Opposite bottom - *One of the periodic refuges is well illuminated by the superb lighting effects.*

Pages 40 & 41 *- Water borne minerals have glued the remaining ballast together. Collars of brickwork serve as reminders of regular repair works.*

***Top -** In an equally delightful setting lies the southern exit of Combe Down tunnel. Standard Class 4 76010 emerges from the tunnel with a 3 coach local in the last few months of the line's existence. Emerging into the fresh air was always a welcome experience for the footplate crew after the smoky confines of the narrow tunnel bore. (JG)*

***Left -** Nature is encroaching onto the former trackbed and presents quite a contrast from the view of the tunnel above and as shown on page 116 of "**Sabotaged & Defeated – Revisited**" (JG)*

VALE OF MIDFORD

Top - *The sinuous nature of the line hereabouts is evident in this view looking towards the viaduct at Midford. (JG)*

Bottom - *A view across the valley to Midford Castle with the S&D track bisecting the panorama. The stubble fields lying below the castle were captured on film on a glorious October day in 1964. (BIT)*

Top - *The yard crane and the loading gauge perfectly frame this view of the entrance to Midford Goods Yard, which had been closed in June 1963, in this view taken in March 1966 at the very end of the line's life. (BIT)*

Bottom - *A 1974 view of the remains of Midford Goods yard where the concrete stand for the yard crane is still evident. Eight years after closure the formation of the line is now but a grassy track passing to the left side of the row of fence posts. (SC)*

Top - *Looking south through Long Arch bridge in the last month of the line's existence. (BIT)*

Right - *A strikingly lit shot of a train on the narrow ledge upon which the single track makes its way northwards from Midford station. The locomotive is 76026 with the 12:05 service from Templecombe photographed on the 3rd December 1965 the last month of full services prior to the introduction of the "Emergency Timetable". (DF)*

MIDFORD

Top - *73001 has now traversed Devonshire and Combe Down tunnels and has just passed Midford station as it crosses Midford Viaduct at the head of the 09:53 from Bath Green Park to Bournemouth train on 23rd December 1965. The line opened out to double track from here southwards to Templecombe and at this point the old GWR Limpley Stoke to Camerton line passed underneath, the abandoned trackbed seen crossing from left to right. (GP)*

Bottom - *The Midford signalman leans out to hand over the single line token to the driver of 76026 about to stop in the station at 13:30, if running to time, with the 12:05 from Templecombe on 3rd December 1965. (DF)*

Opposite top - *34057 "Biggin Hill" runs tender first over Midford viaduct on the morning of 5th March 1966 en route to Evercreech Junction to double head in company with 34006 "Bude" the LCGB "Somerset & Dorset Railtour". The crew keep a sharp lookout always a difficult task running backwards with a tender locomotive. (JG)*

Opposite bottom - *An atmospheric view of the interior of the signalbox taken in the late afternoon of Sunday 6th March 1966, the last day that trains ran on the line. The interior of the box has been recreated at Washford on the West Somerset Railway by the Somerset & Dorset Railway Trust. (N McC)*

13
OVER
LOCKED
TO
15
FREE
TO
STARTER
FROM
13
15
16
15
16

Top - *A scheduled stop to surrender the single line tablet turned into a protracted photographic stop at Midford as the very last southbound passenger train over the S&D pauses on Sunday 6th March 1966. It is 17:30 and dusk is fast approaching as 34013 "Okehampton" with 34057 "Biggin Hill" behind await the return of the train's photographers who attempt to record the scene in the fast fading light. The electric headlamps of the pacific stand out in the gloom as do lights in the signalbox adding atmosphere to this historic scene and an hour later the final northbound special would pass through. The progress of the southbound special near Masbury was unforgettably captured in words by Robin Atthill in his book* **"The Somerset & Dorset Railway"....... "As dusk fell on the evening of Sunday 6 March 1966 two Southern Pacifics stormed their way up to Masbury summit with their nine-coach special. I watched the red tail-lamp of the train disappear into the darkness. Only a minute before I had seen a glowing pillar of fire racing through Binegar; little flames flickered on embankments that were still sodden after six inches of rain in the last month**." (JG)

Below - *Smoke rises from the chimney of the pub directly below the viaduct rather than from a steam locomotive approaching Midford station. The demolition contractors had reached Midford late in 1967 and this bleak scene was captured shortly thereafter (BIT)*

Top right - *The initial preservation attempt, of the three so far made at this site, saw the laying of narrow gauge tracks from the platform for some distance towards Tucking Mill Viaduct in the 1980s. Known as The Tucking Mill Tramway, a handcrafted sign adorns the track which was of two foot gauge. A number of trucks from the Monkton Farleigh underground ammunition store were in use here. Unfortunately the scheme failed and the tracks were subsequently removed. (SC)*

Bottom right - *The locomotive used for a short time on the tramway was a Simplex named "Adam". Formerly housed at the Cotswold Wildlife Park Railway, it was disguised with bodywork shaped to look like a GWR pannier tank. It is here seen being loaded onto a low loader following cessation of activities at the site in 1987. (SC)*

***Top -** The latest manifestation of preservation seen at Midford, following the initial scheme illustrated on the previous page and the subsequent scheme, illustrated on page 131 of **"Sabotaged & Defeated – Revisited":** both failed. The New Somerset & Dorset Railway Society has started work on making Midford into a preservation base and they also hope to take over restoration of Spetisbury station in the near future. The results of their clearance work at Midford are evident in this view. The intention is to rebuild Midford station in 1950s/1960s style with the building serving as an office, shop, refreshment room and information point for the whole route. (JG)*

***Right -** Having just passed the 40 mph speed restriction sign double track will shortly come to an end as 76026 is about to enter the single line section to Bath Junction with the 12:05 service from Templecombe on 2nd December 1965. (DF)*

Top - *The attractive 4 span viaduct to the north of Wellow station seen in 1966. Smoke from a bonfire drifts lazily across this bucolic panorama enhanced as it is by cows grazing contentedly in a nearby field. Rather than intruding into the landscape the viaduct and railway embankment very much enhance the pastoral scene. (JG)*

Bottom - *A seemingly deserted Wellow plays host to 82041 as it restarts the 13:10 from Bath on 13th October 1965. (DF)*

***Top** - Standard Class 3 tank 82030 stops at Wellow on the 8th December 1965 in the aftermath of a rainstorm as witnessed by the wet platforms and rainbow. The train is the 13:10 from Bath to Templecombe. (RP)*

***Bottom** - Arriving from the south on 13th October 1965 is 80138 with the 12:05 from Templecombe to Bath. Running time from Wellow to Bath was 18 minutes for the 6¾ mile run into the Georgian city. What would the inhabitants of this still relatively isolated community give for such a service today? (DF)*

***Opposite top** - Following closure the station was bought and converted into a house. In this 1972 view the owner, Peter Blake, later Sir Peter Blake, can be seen enjoying the view from the platform shaded from the August sun by the canopy. The grassed-over space between the tracks where trains once ran now houses swings and a climbing frame for the children of the house to enjoy. (MSH)*

***Opposite bottom** - The original station building on the left has been linked to a new building on the right to provide enlarged accommodation. (MSH)*

Against threatening skies 82030 gets away southwards from Wellow in this atmospheric view, sleepers from the lifted goods yard, closed in June 1963, being evident on the right. (RP)

SHOSCOMBE & SINGLE HILL HALT

Top - *About to pass over the 7 span Home Farm viaduct near Shoscombe is the 12:05 from Templecombe headed by 76026 on 10th December 1965. (DF)*

Bottom - *The structure of the halt is revealed in this 1972 view, the concrete harp and slab construction being evident. Being integral to the halt both nameboards survive some six years after closure. (MSH)*

L 16VB
are 7-16
3038

STONE TRAFFIC ONLY
FROME TO BRACKNELL

WRITHLINGTON

A spot of bother at Writhlington sidings as Class 08 shunter D3003 has managed to become derailed on 1st July 1969. A group of railwaymen stand around, looking rather perplexed as to what to do next. (DF)

RADSTOCK NORTH

Opposite top *- This view of Writhlington shows clearly the colliery winding gear, one wheel of which has subsequently been placed in Radstock town centre near the site of Radstock North station. (MSI)*

Opposite bottom *- The few coal trucks in the siding on the right give the lie to this view which with its rusting track and general air of decay might be thought of as depicting a closed railway. In fact this shot was taken on 17th August 1972, over a year before closure of the colliery saw the end of freight services over the final section of the S&D. (MSH)*

This page *- Jinty 47506 has charge of the Radstock shunting duty on 1st December 1965. (DF)*

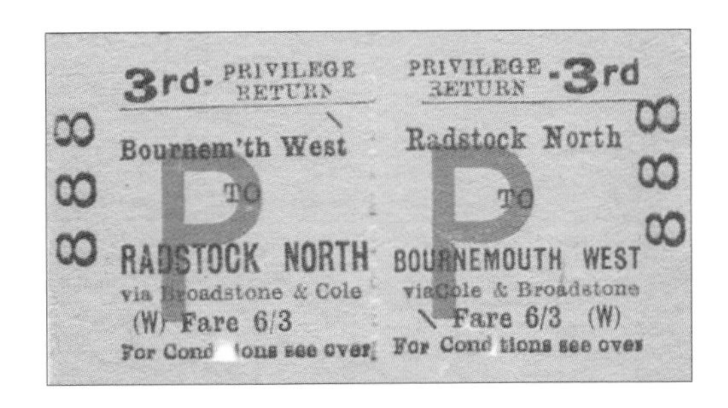

47276

Opposite top - *Against a background of slagheaps so untypical of rural Somerset a couple of Jinties, 47276 and 47506, can be seen near Radstock sub shed. (DF)*

Opposite bottom - *A close up of the stone built engine shed at Radstock a sub shed of Bath. It is seen here apparently devoid of life on 17th July 1965. (DF)*

This page - *A March 1973 view of the shed with the preservation society's rake of coaches seen to the right and Jinty 47493 recently arrived from Barry scrapyard occupying one of the shed roads. At this time the shed was shared with BR's own resident Class 08 shunter. The Jinty was towed to Westbury in November 1973 and taken on to Cranmore (and subsequent restoration) by David Shepherd's Standard 75029 en route from Eastleigh. It returned to S&D metals 32 years later in July 2005 when it visited Midsomer Norton preservation site. (MSI)*

Top - *Covered with tarpaulins the preserved S&D 7F 53808 finds shelter inside Radstock shed together with a BR Class 08 diesel. 53808 spent six years at Radstock before the scheme here failed and it moved to the West Somerset Railway where it was fully restored. (JG)*

Bottom - *Class 08 shunter D3750 is seen outside Radstock shed on the occasion of a Somerset & Dorset Trust steam day held on Easter Monday 1973. Writhlington Colliery was to close later that year and the stock of the society subsequently transferred away to Washford on the West Somerset Railway. (JG)*

Top - *Running in to Radstock, past a reasonably well filled goods yard, with the 09:00 from Bristol to Bournemouth on 1st July 1965 is 73054. (DF)*

Bottom - *Seen from a similar viewpoint but this time on 4th September 1967, some 18 months after closure, a pair of NB Type diesels, D6331 and D6311, have just crossed to the up line in preparation for heading south with two brakevans in tow to collect the rake of trucks containing recovered materials brought to the interchange point for crews at Evercreech Junction, the railhead at this time being at Templecombe. (DF)*

Top - *On 11th October 1965 73001, which was to disgrace itself by failing at Midsomer Norton as detailed in **"Sabotaged & Defeated - Revisited"** a few weeks later, has no problems with the 13:10 Bournemouth to Bath service as it makes its exit from Radstock. (DF)*

Bottom - *80043 awaits the "right away" with the 15:20 train from Bath to Templecombe on 10th December 1965. This Standard tank was to run right up to the last day, 5th March 1966, when it took out the final 16:25 departure from Bath. (DF)*

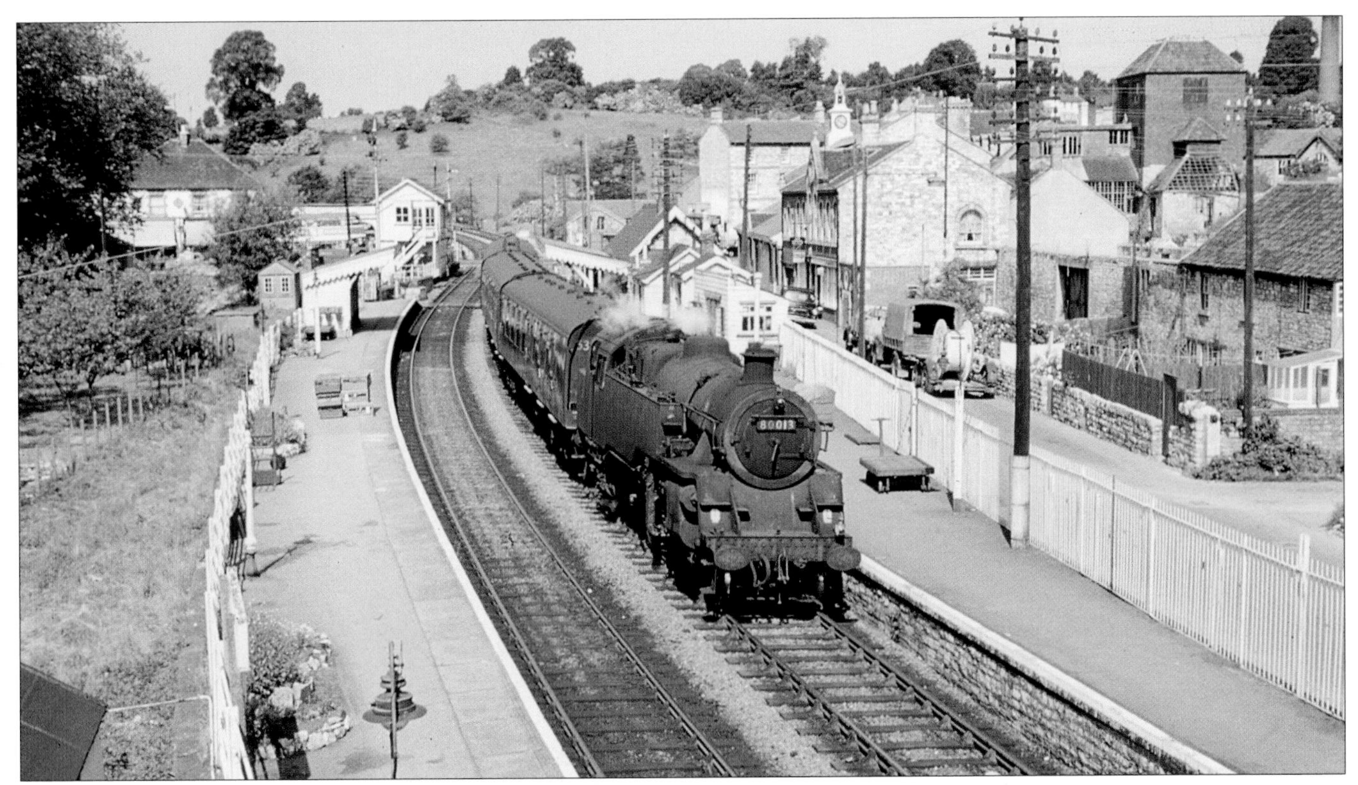

Top - *Standard class 4 tank 80013 enters Radstock with the 09:05 service from Templecombe on 1st July 1965, a lovely summer's morning. Some interesting boxes await collection by the next southbound service on the down platform, which is headed* ***(bottom)*** *by one of the S&D's stock of Standard Class 5s, 73054, on the 09:00 Bristol - Bournemouth service. Three of this type were allocated from new to Bath in 1954 and proved very successful. 73054 was a later allocation, not arriving at Bath until April 1961. (Both: DF)*

Top - *47544 waits in Radstock station with empties for Writhlington Colliery on 12th October 1965. (DF)*

Bottom - *80041 enters Radstock with the 11:46 from Bournemouth on 3rd December 1965 passing 47506 at the down platform with empties for Writhlington Colliery. (DF)*

Opposite top - *A view of a departing southbound service beginning the 1 in 50 climb out of Radstock in late 1965. The locomotive has just passed over the bridge which formerly crossed the track of the old Welton tramway. (CB)*

Opposite bottom - *The RCTS special of 2nd January 1966 sees 34015 "Exmouth" piloted by U Class 31639 flashing across Radstock level crossing. The tour was limited to 10 coaches although demand far outstripped available seats, the tour being run on what was thought to be the last day of operation of the line. In the event however, the line remained open for a further two months due to delays in licensing replacement bus services. (DF)*

D7039
7V40

RADSTOCK
NORTH

Opposite top - *D7039 prepares to set out from Radstock station with the first train over the S&D since closure. On Sunday 18th September 1966 this special working was run to allow demolition contractors who wished to tender for the work the opportunity to inspect the line and the scale of the work involved. The successful tenderer turned out to be W.R. Arnott, Young & Co. of Bilston, Staffordshire who were awarded the contract for the section from Blandford to Radstock in December 1966, work beginning a mile north of Blandford in February 1967. (DF)*

Opposite bottom - *On 4th September 1967 a demolition train returns from Evercreech Junction with D6331 double heading D6311 into Radstock North station. These North British machines would be replaced by Hymeks by the end of the year. (DF)*

Right top - *The following day, another pair of North British Type 2s (later TOPS class 22), running wrong line, rumble through an increasingly dilapidated Radstock station on their way to Evercreech Junction to collect their train of recovered materials on 5th September 1967. (DF)*

Right middle - *A BR Class 08 shunter is seen with a couple of oil tank wagons and a Presflo vehicle crossing the S&D level crossing into Radstock North station in 1970. The driver of the first car in the queue - a Hillman Hunter - seems to have disappeared and the car boot is open so perhaps he was in for a long wait. (SDRHT)*

Right bottom - *An aerial view taken from our intrepid photographer's overnight stop at the Waldegrave Arms in Radstock in August 1972 shows the former Market Hall, now housing a museum, and the crossing gates and station at Radstock North. The remaining freight service to Writhlington colliery had a little over a year left to run before withdrawal and the final closure of the last section of the S&D to remain open. (MSH)*

Top - The RCTS "Thames & Avon" Railtour special of 6th April 1968 enters Radstock station via the new spur line from the North Somerset route en route to Writhlington Colliery. A trainload of enthusiasts hang out of the windows savouring the experience of travelling on S&D metals. (DF)

Below - Consisting of cars 51367/59513/59543/51409 the RCTS DMU tour, which originated from Paddington, is seen passing the Goods Shed en route to Writhlington Colliery at a little after 3pm on 6th April 1968. Prior to this the special had run from Frome to the foot of the incline serving Kilmersdon Colliery in order to reach Radstock. It then ran on to Bristol via the North Somerset line. (JL)

Opposite - Two further views of the RCTS special of 6th April 1968: top, pausing for a photographic stop at Radstock North station and, bottom, heading out to the new spur connection to the North Somerset line and thence to Bristol. (JL)

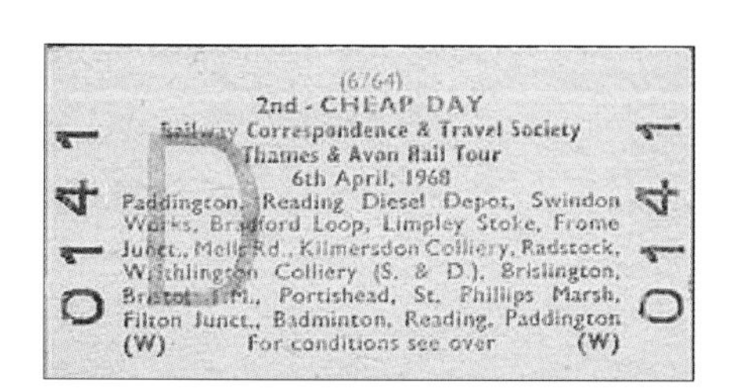

0141 (6/64) 0141
2nd - CHEAP DAY
Railway Correspondence & Travel Society
Thames & Avon Rail Tour
6th April, 1968
Paddington, Reading Diesel Depot, Swindon Works, Bradford Loop, Limpley Stoke, Frome Junct., Mells Rd., Kilmersdon Colliery, Radstock, Writhlington Colliery (S. & D.), Brislington, Bristol T.M., Portishead, St. Phillips Marsh, Filton Junct., Badminton, Reading, Paddington
(W) For conditions see over (W)

Top and opposite top - *Two views of the station in 1972 during its time as a preservation centre with buildings having been spruced up with a coat of paint. (MSI)*

Opposite bottom - *With track lifted Radstock North awaits demolition. In the foreground are the remains of the low bridge that allowed small cars (but neither lorries nor buses) to avoid the sometimes interminable queues that formed when the level crossing gates remained closed for extended periods. (MB)*

RADSTOCK WEST FROME - BRISTOL

Opposite top - *Collecting the token for the North Somerset line is the driver of Hymek D7051 in charge of the afternoon freight to Bristol East Depot on 10th August 1965. (DF)*

Opposite bottom - *A Class 08 Diesel shunter brings another load of Writhlington coal over the ex GWR level crossing at Radstock West in 1972, a year before closure of the colliery. (JL)*

Top and right - *An interesting working is captured at Radstock West as Hymek D7013 worked an inspection saloon from Frome to Bristol over the closed section of route between Mells Road and Radstock on 24th February 1967. As the Frome to Mells Road section was worked on a "One engine in steam" basis the special was worked over this section by two Hymeks, the pilot returning to Frome with the token. (DF)*

Top *- Another inspection train was run on 22nd March 1968 from Frome to Radstock powered by D7043 with inspection saloon W80975. It is captured here near Kilmersdon village with the Hymek propelling the saloon. The timing of this inspection proved fortuitous as, following severing of the North Somerset line by floods on 10th July 1968, the remaining traffic from Radstock would come this way. The double track line between Mells Road and Radstock was reduced to a single operating line, the up line being in use for half a mile from Mells Road where the track was slewed into the down line for the remainder of the journey to Radstock. In any event, it had been the intention to close the North Somerset route from 30th June but this was delayed as the necessary maintenance and S&T work on the Frome line had not been completed. (DF)*

Left *- As at Radstock rail facilities at Midsomer Norton were also shared with the ex-GWR line and here we see Hymek D7000 running through the GWR station with a coal train for Portishead power station on 16th November 1967. (DF)*

KILMERSDON COLLIERY

Having covered both Norton Hill and Writhlington collieries, served by the S&D, in this book and its precursor I thought it only right to include the third of Radstock's remaining pits even though it had been served by the ex GWR line from Frome to Radstock. Output from this mine helped to ensure the rail link via Frome remained open to carry away the coal from Writhlington as the two were linked underground in their later days, all mined coal surfacing at Writhlington, thus it was, effectively, served by the S&D in its final years.

Although BR had indicated in 1968 that the North Somerset coalfield was likely to last "another eight years" it was in fact only to remain operative until 1973. On May 16th of that year the announcement came that both the two remaining collieries, Writhlington and Kilmersdon, would close at the end of September. This was all the more surprising as in the early part of 1973 output from Writhlington had been on the increase. Apparently the problems were not due to any lack of coal reserves nor to the difficulty of working the seams but related to a rapidly declining workforce, the mines attracting less and less people into them by the early 1970s.

Kilmersdon closed in September 1973, shortly before that at Writhlington. I made a visit to the colliery on 5th February 1968 and was fortunate enough to have a ride on the footplate from the mine to the head of the incline.

Kilmersdon Colliery with wooden-bodied railway wagons under the loading gantry on which a small manually operated coal chaldron can be seen on the overhead tramway. (RH)

NCB

Opposite top *- A view down the incline with a full truck descending to the valley below. The incline and tramway had been constructed in 1877, the incline being just over 400 feet in length with double track at the top leading to a single line approximately half way down. The gradient varied from 1 in 4.3 at its steepest to 1 in 9.5 at the foot of the incline.*

Opposite bottom *- An NCB operative handles the levers controlling the incline mechanism as an empty truck appears at the top of the incline.*

This page *- A Peckett 0-4-0ST at Kilmersdon Colliery in 1968 carried Works No. 1788 and was built in 1929. The Peckett is seen in company with an interesting assortment of road vehicles.*

Out of use at the side of one of the coal hoppers was a rather small 1931-built Hunslet 0-4-0T, No. 1684, fitted with a Belpaire firebox and outside Walschaerts valve gear, both items being somewhat rare in British industrial locomotive practice. Passing through several owners it had arrived at Kilmersdon, where it is seen in this view in February 1968, from Norton Hill colliery. It found little work here and departed later in 1968 for preservation, initially at the Somerset Railway Museum located at Bleadon & Uphill station but today it is to be found on the Middleton Railway in Leeds.

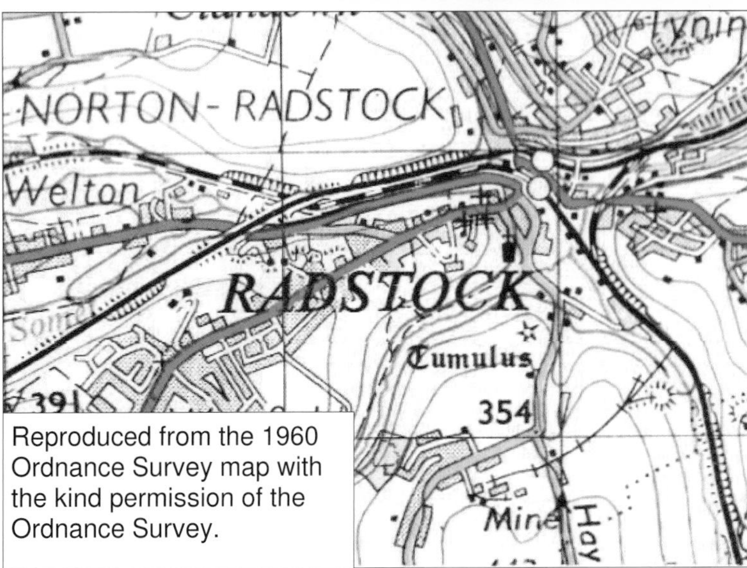

Reproduced from the 1960 Ordnance Survey map with the kind permission of the Ordnance Survey.

Above - *The old road sign for a level crossing featured a steam locomotive which by 1968 was becoming something of an anachronism but which in the case of Kilmersdon still held true until closure came five years later, the line being steam worked until the end.*

Top - *The Peckett collects the empty truck which has just arrived at the top of the incline preparatory to returning it to the colliery.*

Bottom - *Resplendent in red and green the Peckett crosses the road adjacent to the mine propelling its load towards the incline top in 1972. No.1788 was to be preserved on permanent loan from the NCB and arrived at Radstock where there was a fledgling S&D preservation society in June 1974, after having descended the incline and making an appearance at the nearby Camerton traction engine rally in steam on its low loader. Seven 4-wheel open wagons were also acquired from Kilmersdon. Its current home is on the West Somerset. (JL)*

A cabside view taken from the Peckett looking towards the pitwheel and main mine buildings.

All photos in this feature JG except as credited.

EXIT FROM RADSTOCK

A brace of NB Type 2s D6331 and D6323, reverse their train over the connecting spur from the North Somerset line to the S&D on 7th September 1967. (DF)

Top - *With the new connection evident in the foreground Hymek D7041 descends the grade into Radstock with a demolition train on 22nd November 1967 shortly after Hymeks assumed the motive power role from the Class 22s. (DF)*

Bottom - *What turned out to be the last passenger train to traverse the North Somerset line prior to closure by floods near Whitchurch in July 1968. This was the RCTS special (previously seen at Radstock North) of 6th April 1968 seen here just before the Five Arches bridge heading towards Bristol. (DF)*

***Top -** Diesel shunter D3522 propels its train up the gradient to Midsomer Norton passing the connecting line on 5th March 1969 during recovery of the remaining track between Midsomer Norton and Radstock. (DF)*

***Opposite top -** D7031 makes its way to Radstock North and the S&D yard over the connecting spur on 3rd May 1966, a couple of months after passenger closure of the S&D. (DF)*

***Opposite bottom -** Hymek D7011 has just parted company with D7031 which together formed the combined afternoon freight from Bristol East Depot to Radstock. D7031 has just crossed to the S&D yard whilst D7011 will continue into Radstock West. (DF)*

***Left** - In 1968 a Class 08 shunter, D3182 , brings some empty wagons up the North Somerset line before reversing over the new connection, which can just be seen behind the rake of trucks, onto the S&D line. (JG)*

5U21
SW

6H20

Top - *About to cross over the Five Arches or North Somerset Viaduct is D7041 on 22nd November 1967 with a demolition train. Patches of frost or early snow on the embankment give an indication of how cold it was! (DF)*

Bottom - *An August 1972 view from the middle of the track forming the connecting spur showing the formation of the lifted S&D on the right and the shunting neck of the North Somerset to allow movement to Radstock West yard on the left. (MSI)*

Top - *Trundling up the incline to its first stop at Midsomer Norton is the inspection special of 18th September 1966. (DF)*

Bottom - *80013 leaves Midsomer Norton with the 09:05 Templecombe - Bath service on 30th June 1965, passing the milepost recording the fact that the train has another 11.75 miles to run to Bath. (DF)*

Next page - *48760 climbs up the grade to Norton Hill colliery with coal empties on 4th November 1965. Unknown to miners at the time the colliery only had another few weeks of production left before closure in February 1966, a matter of just a few weeks before the closure of the line that served it. (DF)*

48760

BEWARE OF
TRAINS

NORTON HILL COLLIERY

Opposite top - *With the pithead winding gear clearly visible on the right Jinty 47276 busies itself with shunting coal wagons whilst 8F 48706 prepares to move off with its train on 23rd November 1965. Note the mainline running at a considerably lower level on the far left of this view. (DF)*

Opposite bottom - *A footplate view taken from 47276 as 48706 prepares to depart Norton Hill colliery sidings on 23rd November 1965. (DF)*

NORTON HILL COLLIERIES COMPANY,

RADSTOCK, Somerset.

From Norton Hill Sidings, Midsomer Norton (S. & D.)

To BATH (M.R.)

For the Bath Gas Company.

No. Date 191

Trucks detained longer than 24 hours after arrival will be charged at the rate of 3/- per day.

Bottom - *Hunslet 0-4-0 No. 1684 is seen at work in the colliery sidings on 1st July 1965 drawing out loaded coal wagons for collection by BR motive power. Upon closure of the colliery the locomotive was transferred to the nearby Kilmersdon pit (see page 79). The NCB sidings which No.1684 was working were on the level in contrast to the S&D line in the background which descended to Radstock at a gradient of 1 in 50. The market town of Midsomer Norton can be seen spread out below the railway which was situated on the edge of the hillside. (DF)*

Top *- Passing some industrial plant associated with Norton Hill colliery Jinty 47276 is returning light engine to Radstock on 16th July 1965. (DF)*

Bottom - *The signal is off for a pair of NB Type 2s, D6331 and D6311, as they grind up the incline past the Norton Hill Colliery sidings on the right on 5th September 1967. However, they are working on the former up line, the only one in use for demolition trains at this point. (DF)*

Top - *Passing the same spot as the 'Jinty' opposite, on the single track that then remained, is shunter D3522 with a recovery train on 5th March 1969, the third anniversary of closure of the line to service trains. (DF)*

Bottom - *A little further down the bank the same train makes its cautious descent, passing the vast slagheap on the left. Not long after, recovery of track back to Radstock was completed. (DF)*

73001 descends the incline from Midsomer Norton on the frosty morning of 22nd November 1965 with the 10:14 service to Bath. (DF)

Top - *Passing over Silver Street bridge 73001 is about to stop at Midsomer Norton station with the 09:00 service from Bristol to Bournemouth on a rather warmer 4th November 1965. (DF)*

Bottom - *The signal is off for the 09:05 from Templecombe headed by 82041 on 16th December 1965. (DF)*

82041

Opposite *- Whilst 82041 waits at the platform with the 09:05 from Templecombe - Bath the photographer cabs a ride on Jinty 47276, engaged on shunting Norton Hill colliery sidings, on 23rd November 1965. (DF)*

This page *- A nocturnal view of 82044 getting away from Midsomer Norton with the lightweight 18:05 Bath - Binegar local on the evening of 25th October 1965. A census was undertaken by BR covering the weeks 7th July 1962, 25th August 1962 and 6th May 1963 as part of the run-up to closure and the average passenger loadings on this service made depressing reading. (DF)*

	Joining	Alighting
Bath	18	0
Midford	0	2
Wellow	1	6
Shoscombe	1	5
Radstock	0	4
Midsomer Norton	0	1
Chilcompton	0	1
Binegar	0	1

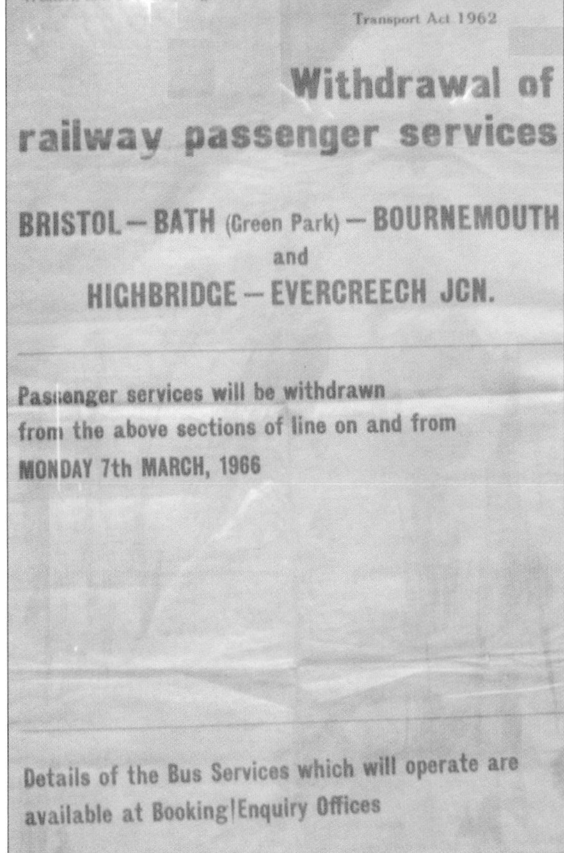

Western and So[illegible]hern Regions

British Railways Board
Transport Act 1962

Withdrawal of railway passenger services

BRISTOL – BATH (Green Park) – BOURNEMOUTH
and
HIGHBRIDGE – EVERCREECH JCN.

Passenger services will be withdrawn from the above sections of line on and from MONDAY 7th MARCH, 1966

Details of the Bus Services which will operate are available at Booking/Enquiry Offices

Top - *The pair of NB Type 2s previously seen on page 92, are depicted here at Midsomer Norton.(DF)*

Bottom - *Hymek D 7039 waits whilst the contractors' representatives cross the tracks during their inspection. (DF)*

Top - *Seen in the winter of 1967 Midsomer Norton South station awaits a renaissance which at that time was considered most unlikely. Today tree cover and housing development obscure the fields seen in the right background, and the buildings of the closed Norton Hill colliery are prominent on the skyline. (Roy Brown courtesy SDRHT)*

Bottom - *Masonry litters the platform of the station building seen here in 1969. (MC)*

Left *- The tall home signal has now been re-erected here by the S&DRHT but, alas, Silver Street bridge is no more precluding any extension towards Bath for the preservationists for the foreseeable future. This view dates from 1969 following removal of the track back to Radstock. (MC)*

Bottom *- Photographed in 1975 at perhaps its nadir, the infilled tracks between the platforms and decrepit wooden shelter show the scale of the challenge which faced the preservationists at this site. (SC)*

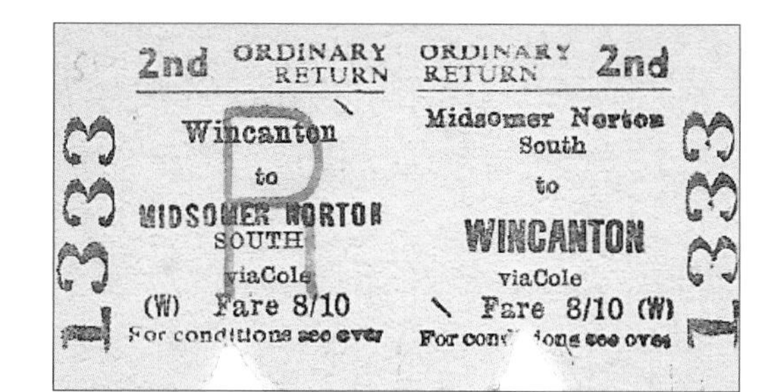

THE S&D TRUST AT MIDSOMER NORTON

Top - View from the new signalbox looking up the double track mainline towards Chilcompton. Hopefully further extensions of track will be made in this direction in years to come. (JG)

Right - A view of the reconstructed greenhouse, always a feature of the S&D at this location, taken from the signalbox, both structures having been lovingly recreated on their original footprints at Midsomer Norton South station. (JG)

Left - *The Sentinel locomotive currently under restoration poses in front of the reconstructed signal box. Manufactured by the Sentinel Waggon Works at Shrewsbury in 1927, Sentinel 7109 is a balanced, double-engined, single-geared, industrial steam locomotive similar to the pair that operated at Radstock. (JG)*

This Class 08, built in 1961 at Horwich, is in fine external condition and liveried in all over BR green, with black and yellow 'wasp' stripes on the front and rear ends and red bufferbeams, and bears its pre-TOPS (BR classification, No. 08881) number of D4095. It arrived on site in January 2012. (JG)

This page - *Arriving at the S&DRHT site at Midsomer Norton at the end of 2011 was a 2 car Class 108 Diesel Multiple Unit built by BR Derby in 1960. Formerly Network South East set L231, it consists of vehicles 51909 and 54271. It came from a previous restoration and storage home at Long Marston and was soon put to use on crew training duties. This may well have been the face of the S&D in the late 1960s had the line been reprieved.*

Top - *A view from the front end of the DMU as it approaches Midsomer Norton station.*

Bottom - *The current limit of track with a working party seen through the front window of the DMU, now offering rides along the short length available. (JG)*

A final reminder of times past at Midsomer Norton, as 73068 storms up the grade with the 09:00 from Bristol on 23rd November 1965, passing 47276 shunting Norton Hill colliery sidings with an 8F at the rear. Another reminder of the past is the town's former gasholder, clearly visible in the valley below. (DF)

CHILCOMPTON

Top right - *Drifting down the grade on the approach to Chilcompton tunnel, passing through some attractive scenery, seen at its best on this July day in 1965, and travelling along immaculately maintained permanent way, is 80043 with the 09:05 from Templecombe to Bath. (DF)*

Middle - *On 28th July 1965 Standard Class 5 73051 has charge of the 09:00 Bristol to Bournemouth service. The red warning boards proclaiming "Stop Look and Listen" are very evident next to the boarded foot crossing at the platform ends, there being no footbridge provided at this location. (DF)*

Bottom right - *Shrouded in escaping steam 82041 departs from the Chilcompton stop on 11th November 1965 with the 09:05 train from Templecombe. Water from the nearby column was not required on this occasion. (DF)*

A close up view of Chilcompton's water crane, which, protected by its wooden casing, has come to the end of its useful life in this post closure view. Neither the leather bag which hangs limply nor the associated "fire-devil", used as an additional frost prevention measure, will be required again. (JG)

Top - *73068 labours up the grade towards a deserted Chilcompton station with the 09:00 from Bristol on 11th November 1965. Rationalisation had proceeded apace with the destaffing of the station in February 1964, closure of the goods yard in June 1964, closure of the signalbox in April 1965 and the lifting of the station sidings and crossover facilities in July 1965.*

Middle - *The staggered platforms at this location, still retaining remnants of flower borders, are apparent in this view of 76026 entering the station with the 09:05 Templecombe – Bath service on 28th July 1965.*

Bottom - *Two years later NB Type 2 diesel no. D6330 passes through Chilcompton station on 15th May 1967 en route to Evercreech Junction to collect a demolition train of recovered materials brought up from the railhead by another crew. The crews of southbound and northbound trains changed at Evercreech Junction. (All: DF)*

***Top** - Chilcompton looms through the mist of the early morning of 23rd November 1967 in this guard's van view at the tail of a demolition train en route to Evercreech Junction on which I was fortunate enough to take a ride. The water crane bag hangs limply on the up platform, a reminder of better days. (JG)*

MOOREWOOD

The inspection special of 18th September 1968 approaches Moorewood headed by D7039 and crosses bridge No. 59 spanning the Bristol road. The white gate in the right background formerly gave access to the Emborough stone crushing plant sidings which were out of use by June 1965. The Emborough Stone Co. Ltd. was registered in 1907 acquiring the business of the quaintly named Somerset Fuller's Earth and Ochre Co. There were two limestone quarries, straddling the S&D line, together with a smaller sandstone quarry just to the north at Emborough Grove. They were particularly well placed to supply roadstone to the Bath area by rail and the two quarries were interconnected by a tramway. It continued to operate until after World War Two but since its closure, it has been used for a variety of purposes including military training, waste recycling and concrete product manufacture. (DF)

Top - *The siding at Emborough could still be seen in situ in 1969, some 3 years after the main line was lifted, the empty trackbed being just visible through the left side of the gate. (MC)*

Middle - *73001 rolls into a deserted Binegar station on the 8th November 1965 with the 09:00 Bristol - Bournemouth service. By this date 73001 carried a white painted number on the smokebox door. (DF)*

BINEGAR

Bottom - *A Hymek waits in the spring of 1968 to collect its train of recovered materials which will be brought from the railhead by a diesel shunter. Hymeks had taken over from NB Type 2s as the primary motive power since the previous November and would continue to work over the S&D until June 1968 when the railhead had reached Moorewood and the contractor's base moved to Midsomer Norton. (JL)*

In 1968 Binegar became the contractors' base and the changeover point from diesel shunter to Hymek power, the Class 08 bringing down materials from the railhead near Masbury for collection by a Hymek onward to Radstock. This view from the guards van of the Hymek's train shows just such an arrival. (JL)

***Top -** With a diesel shunter just visible in the distance Binegar presents the appearance of a working station but sadly the line had been closed for over two years when this view was taken in 1968. Judging by the rust on the rails it does not look as if the crossover was in use at this time. The shunter was usually parked in the down refuge at the south end of the station at the conclusion of each day's work. The Stationmaster's house is seen on the left behind the main station building. (SDRHT)*

***Bottom -** Having recently replaced D3805 diesel shunter D3505 marshalls a train at Binegar for waiting Hymek D7028 to take onwards to Radstock on 21st April 1968. (DF)*

Top *- The Inspection train of 18th September 1966 being propelled back to Radstock through the station at Binegar. (DF)*

Middle *- Demolition work has begun on the signalbox at Binegar in this view taken whilst the crew of Hymek D7028 chat with other BR staff on 21st April 1968. The remaining buildings at Binegar would survive only a few weeks longer before demolition. (DF)*

Bottom *- Only the platforms remain adjoining the grass grown former trackbed in this view taken on 30th April 1977. Today a house occupies the site. (PR)*

MASBURY

Top - *80037 tackles the climb to Masbury summit with the 08:15 from Bath on 10th December 1965. (DF)*

Bottom - *At the same location, as evidenced by the distinctive trees on the left, but 17 months later, D6330 with a couple of brakevans in tow climbs to Masbury en route to Evercreech Junction on 15th May 1967. (DF)*

Top - *During the summer of 1967 this NB type 2 diesel locomotive, latterly Class 22, was captured in Masbury cutting with a demolition train. (Roy Brown, courtesy SDRHT)*

Middle - *Departing from lonely Masbury Halt, having no doubt neither collected nor deposited any passengers, 80041 heads off with the 13:10 from Bath to Templecombe on 12th November 1965. This was one of three southbound services serving the halt at this time. (DF)*

Bottom *- A 1972 view of Masbury with grass grown trackbed. (MSI)*

WINSOR HILL TUNNEL

Top - *A thin film of rust on both running lines dates this view to after closure but before the operation of the demolition trains. April 1968 saw the removal of track in this area as the demolition gangs moved northwards. The new tunnel on the former up line was noticeably shorter than the original bore. (JG)*

Middle - *A wintry scene taken from above the northern portal of Winsor Hill tunnel in 1967. The old former signalbox built entirely of stone dates from 1892. Four navvies were killed by a rockfall whilst working on the tunnel in 1873 and were interred in Shepton Mallet cemetery. (Roy Brown courtesy SDRHT)*

Bottom - *Rose bay willowherb flourishes at the northern portals of the twin bores. Shortly after its closure, the Down tunnel was used to test Concorde's Rolls Royce engines. In 1968, steel doors were attached for this purpose and, three years later, a sign warned people to stay out because of possible contamination from "radioactive oil". In 1981 planning permission was granted for the tunnel's conversion into nuclear bunkers, although this lapsed without being exercised. The doors were removed in 1990 and today both bores remain accessible. (JG)*

SHEPTON MALLET (CHARLTON ROAD)

***Top -** A memory of the days of double heading of long summer expresses over the line as 75023 double heads an unidentified Standard Class 5 over Shepton Mallet's graceful Charlton Road curving viaduct of 27 arches. (RH)*

***Left -** 80059 approaches Shepton Mallet with the 3 coaches forming the 15:20 Bath – Templecombe train on 12th October 1965. (DF)*

***Bottom -** This view dates from September 1963 and depicts 53808 taking water at Shepton Mallet whilst working a freight down to Evercreech Junction. That Bentley in the yard looks rather familiar…. (RP)*

Top right - *Enveloped in escaping steam 80037 enters Shepton Mallet with the 08:15 from Bath on 29th December 1965. (DF)*

Top left - *Seen from the carriage window of a southbound service Standard 75009 runs light engine tender first through Shepton Mallet having assisted 73054 over the Mendips with a Whit Monday excursion on 7th June 1965. (RP)*

Bottom - *Green liveried Standard Class 3 82001 prepares to depart from Shepton Mallet with a Templecombe service. 82001 lasted in service on the S&D until December 1965. (RH)*

Chris Newman, who now lives in China, recalls the bitter winter of 1962/3 in these views of Shepton Mallet under snow. Snow has drifted up against the platform edges with the ground signals barely showing above the covering of snow. Station staff undertake snow clearance duties at the far end of the southbound platform. (Chris Newman courtesy SDRHT)

*Jinty 47539 has charge of the snowplough with the assistance of a Standard and a Collett Goods coupled behind. The signal is stubbornly stuck at danger due to the icy conditions. Chris had started his journey from Bason Bridge (see page 21/36 in **Sabotaged & Defeated – A Final Glimpse Part 2**) that morning but the train got no further than West Pennard before drifts barred its onward path. Resorting to shanks's pony Chris then walked to Shepton along the A361 where he took these stunning shots. He recalls his disappointment when he got to Shepton to find that no trains were running but this was short-lived because it wasn't long before the snow plough arrived and gave a vivid demonstration of its driving force by rushing back and forth through the station (blasting snow everywhere) and thence over the viaduct and up the hill beyond, getting stuck and having to repeat the exercise. (Chris Newman courtesy SDRHT)*

Top - *Little is left at Shepton Mallet apart from the platforms in this 19th August 1972 view. The whole site was cleared later that year for redevelopment. (MSI)*

Bottom - *Looking south from Shepton Mallet in August 1972 the first overbridge carried the former Cheddar Valley line which, following closure to passengers in 1963, continued to handle stone traffic from nearby Doulting Quarry until 1969. (MSI)*

Top - *Looking northwards from the cutting to south of the GWR crossing of the S&D in this 1977 view the rock and stone faced cutting wall to the right is evident. (PR)*

CANNARD'S GRAVE

Right - *In the summer of 1972 grass grows rank on the former trackbed at Cannard's Grave cutting which was subsequently infilled to bridge height. (MSI)*

Next two pages:

Left top - *A closer view of the two twin arched bridges near Cannard's Grave cutting seen in 1969. These have since been buried by infilling of the cutting. (MC)*

Left bottom - *The drainage channel evident in the middle of the formation in the previous view can be seen in this snowy scene at Cannard's Grave cutting taken on 28th December 1964 from the rear carriage of the northbound 11:40 Bournemouth – Bristol train hauled by 75072. It is apparent just how this cutting was a hazard in times of snow, often being blocked by drifts several feet deep. (TC)*

Right top - *75072 accelerates downhill from Cannard's Grave towards Shepton Mallet. The hardy photographer leaning out of the carriage window has managed to capture the stark beauty of the line in the depths of winter. (TC)*

Right bottom - *75072 tackles the 1 in 50 climb between Evercreech New and Shepton Mallet as it passes over the graceful viaduct at Prestleigh on 28th December 1964 with the 11:40 Bournemouth – Bristol train. (TC)*

PRESTLEIGH VIADUCT

EVERCREECH NEW

Top and middle - *Two views of the Inspection special of 18th September 1966 at Evercreech New. Contractors' representatives have disembarked onto the platform to inspect the demolition work required at this location. (DF)*

Bottom - *Literally the end of the line for the station building, the roof of which is in the course of demolition. The up platform shelter had been previously sold and the Goods Shed demolished in 1968. This view dates from January 1969. (MC)*

Top left - *Bridge No.105 Pecking Mill Viaduct seen in 1972 after removal of the wrought iron girder span across the main Shepton Mallet to Evercreech road. (MSI)*

Top right - *Pecking Mill curve, looking south from Bridge 107, had a 25 mph speed restriction placed upon it and is seen in this 1972 shot with a wooden building erected on the former trackbed. Note the refuge in the wall just to the right of the building. (MSI)*

Middle - *Looking north around the sharp Pecking Mill curve in 1988 the wooden building featured above can still be seen in the distance. (JG)*

Bottom - *All that is left at the actual junction – the Guards' cabin and messroom. Hard to believe that a railway ever ran across this rural pasture such is the scale of the transformation here. We are looking towards the turntable and the Highbridge line. (JG)*

Left *- Standard tank 82011 pauses at Wellow with a southbound Templecombe train.*

Rear cover -
This early 1966 view looking north along the manicured ballast of the "permanent" way near Midford gives no indication that the line was to close in a few days time. (BIT)

Don't forget the previous volume!

The late lamented Somerset & Dorset Railway as you have never seen it before. Not a 'then and now' book, but instead a selection of carefully chosen images depicting the railway in its very last months, weeks and even days of life. The trains, the stations and the people. What makes this series so different is the way author Jeffery Grayer has successfully combined the story to include colour views of the demolition as well.

SABOTAGED & DEFEATED
Revisited

Casebound 99% colour.
136 pages

ISBN 978-1-906419-44-8